Under the Aleppo Sun

ALICE ATTIE

Under the Aleppo Sun

LONDON NEW YORK CALCUTTA

Seagull Books, 2018

Text © Alice Attie, 2018

ISBN 978 0 8574 2 548 5

British Library Cataloguing-in-Publication Data
A catalogue record for this book is available from the British Library.

Typeset by Seagull Books, Calcutta, India
Printed and bound by Maple Press, York, Pennsylvania, USA

for you, dear friend,

who walked the streets of Aleppo with me

Children picking up our bones
Will never know that these were once
As quick as foxes on the hill

Wallace Stevens

Anatomies

Slow the pomegranate ripens.

Slow the disappearing.

If I cannot find you,

I will write you into existence.

Infinite and Finite

We are transparencies, fleshed into the world.
We ask how far can we go before our dreams take shape,
before our ghostly selves transfigure into presences.
We will utter them, as the truths or
the untruths of the imagination.

We are as ruddy as the sun, as moody as
the moon as it glides into the visible.
Faceless in our dreams, we wake to translate,
to consider being, to hold it and not to linger before
the knowledge of our disappearance.

We are atoms; our bones frame us in certitude.
Our blood runs alluvial,
flowing into the possibilities of ourselves.
We are torqued, spreading into such configurations
as we make and unmake in a day, in a year.

We come into speech as we come into silence.
Our breath will shape and loosen and shape
the intimacies of our birthed and dying selves.
From transparencies to form, we are ephemera
turning and returning as the day turns on its axis.

As ruddy as the sun, as moody as the moon,
we are fleshed in radiance and in darkness,
standing, falling and dissolving into the ether, into the
sky's hue as it runs as blue or mournful as the elegies
named and sung in its fading.

But for the Butterflies in Hell

The body in pain
weighs nothing when the air lifts it.

A letter comes
from you

as anonymous
as

the day
it bends into.

I press it.
I furrow it into the spine of a book.

I weave
your pain

into the folds.
It will silence the language of our longing.

Colour the Longing

I see you each morning in the window
of the old shop on the square.
You pile the scarves by colours where they
catch the light, damascene and hued.

Waving in the air, they float luminous as clouds.
You stand against the glass with your broad grin.
Your daughter's photograph is on your phone.
She wears pink and pink her slight smile.

We stood in front of the forbidden synagogue.
We were two.
We sat on the bench.
It was March under the Aleppo sun.

Almonds and Milk

A silver frog with amber eyes,
You held it with your crooked finger.

Here is a gift, you said, *take it for good luck.*

These are

       shards

           for the alphabet of the imagination.

A silver frog with amber eyes,
You held it with your crooked finger.

In the Guise of Beauty

Her pink dress floats above the ocean.
It is a pink bird trembling its wings.

Lifting its tiny body into the barren air,
it catapults the invisible, billowing.

A piece of thought comes to me.
It is so small, I let it slip away.

Into Oblivion

our bodies
amid the flecks

glow
amid the fragments

curl
in patterns

push
the air

luminous
against the firmament

we let go our human selves
to bend

to fall into it
we let go our human selves

Elsewhere

The bells of the salvation army are tolling.
It is almost Christmas.

> *She was looking at the camera.*
> *Her legs were crossed.*

We trudge the avenues with shopping bags,
sometimes stumbling, somethings falling.

We can rub out the memory.
We can make and unmake a space to dissolve in.

> *Your finger is in the heart box.*

To think is white.
Not to think is black.

> *Excruciating, the facts.*

Memory is a Tunnel You Travel

I write to you in ciphers
They are infinite in number.

I set them down as a scrawl,
imagining their confluence as a form of knowledge.

Our stories no longer multiply.
We are silenced, one darkness overcoming another.

As I close my eyes, your face comes to me
as candlelight that filigrees the room.

It is a blue murmur that glows and fades.
I can hear you vanishing.

Slow whispers

I am here

I am not here

There is nothing left, nothing to behold,
nothing for us to tunnel into.

Goodbye dear one.

Honour the Little Ones

The moon

        hangs in the cavity of the night sky
        a dismembered eye.

There are hornets in the eaves.
They sound their plaintive cries.

        Ancient is the humming.
        Ancient the grief.

He comes to her in the guise of a hornet.
He flies into her.

        Ancient their touch.
        Ancient the twisted limb.

The hornet falls.
The child falls.

        Ancient is war.
        Ancient the eyes plucked in sunlight.

The moon

        slow trots the solitary dance of itself
        across the night.

Other Worlds

A squirrel scratches the door of the house in a frenzy
    of confusion.
Its failure is portioned out, silhouetted in the landscape.

The hours spin raucous in their orbits.
The pine needles scatter, dry as nettles under our feet.

We think of another time when our coats were zipped,
when lights wove their belts into our bedrooms.

Where are you? Do you hear the children,
their wild bodies dropping into silence?

Of Zatar and Cherries

We walk the silk souk. Its latticed light a pattern on our faces.

A cafe in the centre of the city is festooned with his portrait.

A book by a young poet stirs you to tears.

Someone is calling your name.

Splashing in puddles are the children.

Schubert's Quintet at the heart strings.

Pins, their pink heads mark your place on the map.

We Mark the Place

We count our steps to pass the time.
The fortuneteller turns the cards.

> sometimes words
> sometimes none

She shuffles the odds.

> she thinks
>> *Existence is where the light is.*

> she thinks
>> *It is what fails the imagination.*

Quickens the Surface

I approach him,
a man in the weight of his thought.

I see him dim in the darkness pending.
He is a man I have composed in the likeness of another.

I greet the awning of his head,
asking time of day, time of year.

A catastrophe might come,
as the grassy waves of spring come.

We are two under a dimpled sky. It halos
oak and sycamore. It feathers the tufted hills.

The river is as brisk as the landscape it mirrors.
We can slip down and wade our bellies to the sky.

We can arrange ourselves in a distance we cannot breach,
to be as fleeting as clouds are white against grey.

It is as if to name our common oblivion is to know that
sea and grass and sky are one.

It is as if something brushed against the leg,
as if we could touch the pathos we lean into, as if

Not to have heard a bird call nor seen the flutter of a wing is
To heave insect and animal into the woods of the imagination,

or to see a man lug his way through the tall greens
with his feet stepping into the perch of his possibility is

to become the gaze that fixes him and feel the heavy labour
      of his movement
as he circles, as he measures two shadows spinning into the arc
      of one.

Obsequies

The heart is its own metaphor.

As thunder works its drumming across the fields,
it shutters the air, tosses the feathers of the smallest bird.

There are no blues no reds to bind the image.

The day lets its curtain down.
From this ledge overlooking one reality, comes another.

We search for the halves and wholes of our severed selves.

Thresholds

Fog dissipates the fields.

Trees stand attentive to the weathering.

They are gnarled into shapes that mimic us.

We are flung into the tempest of our times.

Our bags are full of sorrow.

We Live and Die Counting

Men on benches
finger worry beads, yellows and greens.

On and on and on,
they move their fingers along the beads.

One man looks at us.
He keeps his fingers moving.

You step into the afternoon to peer at the sky.
Bombs come as sunlight comes.

In the equation of death,
light and ruin are one.

The Remains of Things

Flip flops

       on streets

              are strewn like dead birds.

I have left you by the side of the road,
a clay vessel, cracked and scattered.

Flip flops

       on streets

              are strewn like dead birds.

       a frog with amber eyes

              a pink dress

                  a finger

Mother Tongue

You have read books.
You have read Kant and Foucault.

One mind follows another.
They add to the sum of being.

We move through the fluency of language.
Our etymologies are conjugates for the eye.

They are indigo arias intoned in an afterglow.
It is as if the imagination itself was choired for

what we cannot say
what we cannot write

We laugh and cry as if there were no speech,
as if truth could be sketched, azure and cerulean.

One mind follows another.
They add to the sum of being.

Under the Aleppo Sun

An idea pokes its way through a field of golden rod.
It is the *click click* of the cricket,

an anatomist in dry heat that crawls the earth's
pulp while the cries of the woman

who picks her way through the rubble
rise through the blues and pinks of childhood.

She culls, bending and searching, and
in the heap of her gathering, she finds

a small incomprehensible thing.
It is a figure real or imagined.

In the distance, a dreamer slacks in the dream chair.
He hears sounds pierce the misted air.

Is it the little anatomist who *clicks* and *clicks*,
or the woman who whimpers in the aftermath?

They are as undivided as day is from night.
They are subjects in the subject of their worlds.

These Phases

The earth will eclipse the moon.

We will lay down.

We will watch a vanishing cross the sky as spectacle.

One disappearance over another takes precedent.

The proximate fades in quantities of more and most.

Our bodies, as petals of the rose, fall.

If we could climb into the beam of this.

If we could measure our astonishment in verse and in song.

If we could.

What the Season Writes

Leaves descend to darkened hues.

As they sliver the light,

birds are pushed to one side.

They swell in the eye's periphery.

The facts are brown and russet.

They are cattails in the setting of the sun.

Transport

Kneeling by the stone's edge, the grass thins to
meet the granite face where they pause in the noonday sun.
In procession, they circumvent the rock. In succession,
in elegance, they transport their dead to the loam.

It is an illusion, this analogy, conflating these gestures
where we lean, disparately similar, and uncover a likeness,
inching into images of consolation. For our shadows are distinct,
as they hover the mound, as they press into the invisible.

We drop down, our lips quivering and our hearts
half full. Half in triumph, half in catastrophe,
our gaze obviates the days the years the hours. Crawling
the stony ledge, we slip and swerve, turning

slowly into idea and essence, into being, into
knowledge and exhilaration. As the sun declines
its light, our eyes close. In a shiver of warmth, we are
transfigured, perfectly, into one.

What the Eye Beholds

The way the citadel climbs the hill.

The way old men sit on benches and finger worry beads.

The way the scarves of Aleppo flap in the dust.

Forget your children.
If you really want children,
you should make more.
If you don't know how to make more children,
bring us your wives and
we will make children for you.

'Daraa 2011'
Atef Najeeb, cousin of Bashar Al-Assad

Writing

I can bring you closer.
I can tell stories.

The children are playing war games.

> *Bang bang*
> *You're dead.*

A cat limps the mound of ruins.

> *Maybe a child*
> *Maybe a phantom*

You pick among the bones.

> *They are luminous,*
> *Pocked and porous.*

Into the dark pitch of solitude, they dazzle,
pushing pain, until it fits, inexorable, like glove.

On the Balcony Overlooking Al-Jdeyedeh

This idea of existence

like a wave
throws us

brief presences
in

We suck the bone brittle.
We suck the marrow sweet.

This idea of existence

like a wave
throws us

brief presences
in

Being Present

His gaze strays
distracted
whiting of a single eye.

The misted other
in blindness
twitching in the socket.

His slumped shoulders
are quaking, threshing
the air for more.

On mottled legs,
he incites these things
we know ourselves by.

Pigeons and mourning doves
rise, spectral, into
verticals and horizontals,

And we, moaning and
mouthing, stagger,
steady ourselves, and keep moving.

It is Midday in the Middle of a Month
with No Name

They lay in the grief field. The buzz of insects rises and falls.
The trees are withered. The air lets loose its commiseration.

There are children. Their hands
cupping their grins. Their eyes cast down.

It is a simmering day, to see and be seen,
to ask what nudges desire, why the tongue coils and spins.

Here, the heart is submerged and thoughts scatter.
They linger as flies in the mesh of the mind's screen.

She settles in the far field. There comes a poem.
She sees the thing of no thing. It is a thumping in the mind
    with no name.

Listen to the Leaves

A brigade of helicopters tremors in the distance.

I search for you.

        a leaf

            hangs

               the wounded tree

Your tongue croons its lamentation in the wind.

The Hidden are Hidden from View

She sees him in the dark walking.

There is sleep for the sleepers.
There is shelter for the sheltered.

> *intervenes the clucking of a bird*
> *intervenes a howling in the distance*
>
> *ruptures the night*
> *crawls the pavement of her thoughts*

She presses against the pane.
Her body leans into his and shatters it.

The Sacred and the Profane

We watched the young boys playing soccer in the
Umayyad Mosque.
Their cheers rang out as a beautiful call,
the children's call to prayer.

The ball careened across the golden tiles,
In and out of the shadow of the towering minaret,
it bounced like a little planet from their tiny heads.

The elders sat along the sidelines.
They were chatting and nodding,
flinging their chins upwards.

In the golden courtyard of the Umayyad Mosque,
an old ball, deflated, crushed, cavities battered,
was kicked and kicked and kicked again.

Floats the Riverbed

The fish seller looks at me

    I will not say it.

The eyes of dead fish are drained.
They blood-stare into the bucket.

On pellets of ice, their tails
are feathered and splayed.

    Take a photograph, he said

    Of the beautiful fish.

Picking at the Scraps

Our ribs are empty baskets.

the smell of death
at sunrise

no surfaces
no points of meeting

statues made of clay
bodies stiff

We scavenge.

We are worms.
We are rats.

Our ribs are empty baskets.

Triptych with Joseph Beuys

A rabbit hangs in the museum.

Dead pelt against a blackboard,

Its feet are bound.

A hawk casts its shadow.

It climbs an indifference of light and air,

A black form cresting the turquoise.

There are stones placed for the dead.

Children toss them, gaming in the boneyard.

We find them. We tuck them safely in our pockets.

The Spider Sleeps in the Web

It is not as birds in formation claim the air.

It is not meeting you for the first time.

It is not listening to a song so strange so beautiful.

It is not wandering in a city both foreign and familiar.

It is not silence.

It is not writing.

It is not anything.

Repetition and Difference

The scrape of the tire turning
as a bird croons in bruised sunlight.
Pulsing back and forth, the pen
rhythms the plaintive cry,
etched as deep as listening is.

It overhears the world in tatters.
Crouching where we are perched,
from where the bird woos,
our scratch and pull and pluck is
an instant thinking a thought.

In the museum, the horned rhino pauses in
the mourning cage. The dark ripples of the
thickening skin tremble, as if there were a
second dying, as if we could watch the spectacle,
as if the coiffed woman bending her face to the
window names it death in a gasp of recognition.

These Ghosted Demarcations

Count backwards from any number and you
come to zero.

He is a small thing.
He is a fist in my belly.

I carry him in the heartbox.

He measures the quantity of zero.

Because you suffocate.

Because you starve.

I am disfigured in my writing.

Words were written on the walls

Dialogue with Abstraction

he said

I could have seen it coming

she said

you had no idea

he said

we are stunned by the slaughter

she said

this indifference to death

he said

a flood of grief

she said

no expression of sorrow

he says

it all adds up

she says

nothing adds up

We Shape It for the Imagination

Your face in the cafe window reflects
a candle waving its flag against the
glass. It signals comfort, being here
in the sumptuous evening light.

It is a grammar to write ourselves by,
being tangible in the intangible.
We converse, heedless, into the
warmth. We stumble into it.

Sentiment. Possibility.
Swinging back and forth, we can whisper,
murmuring stories, filling spaces,
feathering our hearts.

For desire, poised in the long syllable of speech,
deepens. It flecks our conversation silver, to
loosen, to lift these inklings, to try them,
to strut and stray for their attentions.

We are not forever, she thinks.
We will not endure. These strangers
passing the window is what we are, all.
It will claim us, in the cafe, where it hangs.

As a voice, pitched for an ear, it will
roam and then fall, before we have a chance.
For these fragments dangling from wooden
beams are something to stare at.

We may burrow or curl up inside them,
to sway or turn, as wheels, in the flickering,
in the quaking, to come as evening,
as darkness, comes.

We will not endure.
You are thinking of it, of loving, of living in it.
I follow you with my eyes, and your thoughts,
I see them, shaping my imagination.

An Aleppo Codex

Zigzagging the streets of Aleppo.

The letters are innocent until they stand for it.

A is for abandoned
A is for anguish
A is for atrocities
A is for alone

B is for barrel bombs

C is for cannot see you any more

D is for dreaming
D is for dust

E is for no exit

F is for I have failed you

G is for grieving

H is for homesick

I is for interminable

J is for justice will never

K is for kept in the heartbox

L is for longing

M is for memories

N is for nothing

O is our opening

P is for pieces

Q is for quiet

R is for running among the ruins

S is for scarves waving the air

T is for time has run out

U is for unbearable

V is for vanquished

W is for where are you

X is for eliminated

Y is for you

Z is for zero

Zigzagging the streets of Aleppo.

The letters are innocent until they stand for it.

Still the Landscape

Early this morning,

a breeze on slow feet came,

tentative and shy.

We gathered for conversation but found none.

Melancholy like a great pendulum swings its arc.

The timbers are stacked.

The old barns bend down.

Lullaby

The mind lifts
its wings extended

into the night sky
summoning ideas of infinitude

to assign a word
to assign a meaning

choosing what we say
choosing what we see.

Already this has happened
this beauty in the eyes of the ravaged

this long wandering
this laughter in the distance

the voice of the singer receding
the cyclist riding by

the dragonfly circling
the purple flower bending

trilling its shape
deepening its wilt

tethered to swing
back and forth

to slake each other's thirst
to be each other's shadow.

Elegy

I note a balance in the
flutter of a dead leaf.
The sway of its drift is
a dance in decline towards death.

The eye wants to align,
in the arc of its vision,
the leaf, slipping away,
uplifting into a last breath.

It is a triumph to see what one sees
as the sum of *a* and *b*
or the equation of one dying into another
or a leaf that hangs and falls.

There is no reference for it.
There is nothing to speak of.
It is more than the light it
seeks and dips into, more than

a line of verse balanced in
the articulation of its finitude,
more than the numinous landscape,
more than what shivers and is gone.

Departures

Because we wade into being as into a sea.
Because we steady ourselves in tandem,
tables set, our hearts full.

Because we learn to tongue the impossible,
measuring our proximities in letters,
in books, on walls, in conversation.

Because gravity pulls. We bend into it. We bend
into heaviness, into darkness, into weight,
emptying our sleeves, our pockets.

Because our presences are parallel,
as beams of light, we step into them,
reciprocal, as breath, as becoming.

Because with our bodies centred,
still or wavering, we are framed in languages,
in the poverty and plentitude of speech.

Because one by one, we bend into being.
approaching or retreating, our numbers mount,
climbing the span of a day, a year, a lifetime.

Because we are what we are, wading into
facts and fictions, to claim them, to re-imagine them,
to proclaim, our hearts full, a presence.

•

My four grandparents were born and grew up in Aleppo. In March 2011, I traveled to Syria for the first time. The war was just taking hold, and I spent several weeks in Aleppo, visiting the beautiful city, walking the streets of my ancestors. While I was there, I befriended a young man who owned a small shop not far from my hotel in the Al-Jdeydeh area of the city. I visited with him daily; we talked about much, even the pending disaster, however hushed our discussions were.

In the seven years since my visit, I have tried and failed to reach him, my emails being returned to me each time. These poems, epistolary in spirit, are addressed to this young man and to all those who have survived or perished in the destruction of Aleppo and the horrors of the war in Syria.

I honour the courage of the Syrian people who have struggled and continue to struggle with this unspeakable tragedy.

Acknowledgements

p. 3
'A Postcard from the Volcano'
From Wallace Stevens, *Selected Poems* (John N. Serio ed.).
New York: Alfred A. Knopf, 2009, p. 87.

p. 28
'Daraa's Days of Rage'
First published in Mark MacKinnon, *The Graffiti Kids who Sparked the Syrian War. The Globe and Mail,* Friday, 2 December 2016.

•

The following poems were first published in *H.O.W: An Art and Literary Journal* 13 (Spring/Summer 2017)

'Honour the Little Ones'

'But for the Butterflies in Hell'

'It is the middle of a Month with No Name'

'These Ghosted Demarcations'

'The Hidden are Hidden from View'

With endless gratitude to

my dear mother, Muriel

my children, Justine and Gideon

my partner, Royce

to Naveen Kishore and Sunandini Banerjee
for their friendship, their passionate readings,
their generosity and encouragement

Special thanks to the people and the city of Aleppo